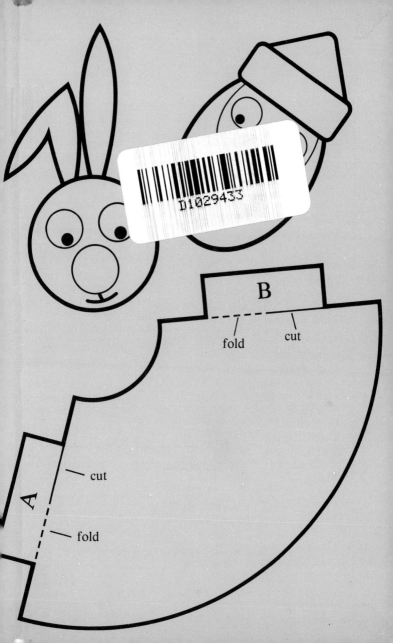

B

fold   cut

cut

A

fold

Contents

Note:

For the purposes of this book, 1 pint (pt) is approximately 500 millilitres (ml) and 1 ounce (oz) = 25 grams (g).

First edition

Party Food

by LYNNE PEEBLES
photographs by TIM CLARK

Ladybird Books Loughborough

Christmas Party

Marzipan Fruits

Peppermint Creams

Christmas Tree

Jacket Potatoes

Snowmen Meringues

Marzipan Fruits

1 Divide the marzipan –
1 piece for each
different type of fruit
being made.

2 Colour each piece by
working a small
amount of food
colouring into the
marzipan. Cut into pieces of the required size.

3 Mould into shapes, add stalks and stems, using
cloves. Add lines on bananas with coffee essence.

Sweets such as these look attractive in small
cardboard boxes lined with a doyley and covered in
cling film.

YOU WILL NEED:

*200 g (8 oz) marzipan –
home-made or bought*

*Food colouring – red,
green, orange, yellow*

*Small paint brush and
coffee essence*

Knitting needle

Cloves

Peppermint Creams

1 Place the egg white in a mixing bowl, whisk until frothy, and add *a few drops* of peppermint flavouring.

2 Work in enough icing sugar to make a stiff mixture. (If food colouring is to be used, add to half or all of the mixture – a pale pink or green is ideal.)

3 Using clean hands knead to a smooth dough, working in more icing sugar if required.

4 Roll out to approximately ½ cm (¼ in) thick, and cut out with sweet cutters. Alternatively, shape into small balls and press out with a fork.

5 Place on a sheet of waxed paper (e.g., the inside liner of a cereal packet) and leave in warm dry place for 24 hours. Store in an airtight tin.

YOU WILL NEED:
1 small egg white
200–300 g (½ – ¾ lb) icing sugar
A few drops of oil of peppermint (or peppermint essence)
Food colouring – pink, green
Sweet cutters

Christmas Tree

YOU WILL NEED:

300 g (12 oz) plain flour
75 g (3 oz) lard
75 g (3 oz) margarine
Level teaspoonful salt
Flour for rolling

4 full tablespoonfuls
  cold water
300 g (12 oz) mincemeat
Beaten egg to glaze
Water (to seal edges)

Icing:
100 g (4 oz) icing sugar
4 × 5 ml teaspoonfuls
  cold water
Glacé cherries

7

1 Make shortcrust pastry as follows. Sift flour and salt into a mixing bowl, add fats cut into small pieces, and rub in with fingertips until mixture looks like breadcrumbs.
Add the water and mix in with a knife, then gather together to make a soft (but not sticky) dough. (It may be easier to gather the dough together in two pieces after the water has been mixed in.)

2 Roll out the dough into two oblongs. Place one piece on a flat baking sheet, then spread mincemeat on it, in the shape of a triangle. Brush 2 cm (¾ in) around mincemeat with water. Place other piece of pastry on top, and cut edges to make branches. Cut small shapes from remaining pastry and decorate. Cut pot and stem. Glaze with egg. Bake 30–35 minutes on Gas Mark 6 (electricity 400°F/200°C). After baking, the tree can be further decorated with glacé icing (see page 42, no. 1 for method) and glacé cherries.

Jacket Potatoes

1 Wash potatoes thoroughly in cold water; dry well. Pierce the skins with a fork in several places.

YOU WILL NEED:

8 medium sized potatoes

1 level teaspoonful salt

2 Place well apart on a baking sheet, and sprinkle with salt.

3 Bake for 1–1½ hours on the middle shelf of a moderate oven, Gas Mark 4 (electricity 350°F/180°C). (The cooking time will vary according to the size of the potato.)

To test when cooked, push a pointed knife into the centre – it should go into the centre easily. Remove from oven, cut a cross in the top and fill as required. (For fillings, see next page.)

9

Bacon & Mushroom Filling (for 4 potatoes)

1 Using a large spoon, remove the hot potato centre and mash well with a fork.

2 Wash and slice mushrooms.

3 Remove rind and chop bacon.

4 Melt margarine on a low heat, add bacon, and fry for 2 minutes.

5 Add mushrooms to pan and fry for a further 2 minutes. Add the mashed potato, and pepper to taste.

6 Place filling in cut potatoes.

YOU WILL NEED:
100 g (4 oz) bacon
100 g (4 oz) mushrooms
25 g (1 oz) margarine
Pepper to taste

Cheese & Ham Filling (for 4 potatoes)

1 Using a large spoon, remove the hot potato centre and mash well with a fork.

2 Mix in the cheese, ham, butter and seasoning.

3 Spoon back into potato shells and serve. (Alternatively, cut potatoes in half lengthwise and serve decorated as shown.)

YOU WILL NEED:
100 g (4 oz) grated Leicester or Cheddar cheese
50 g (2 oz) chopped cooked ham
50 g (2 oz) butter
Salt and pepper

Snowmen Meringues

1 Whisk egg whites until quite stiff. Whisk in 1 tablespoonful sugar, and whisk again.

2 Continue adding the sugar, whisking in 1 tablespoonful at a time. The mixture will become very stiff and almost 'squeaky'.

3 Place small heaps on the lined trays to make bodies. Top with a smaller spoonful for the head.

4 Place trays in oven set at Gas Mark ½ (electricity 250°F/120°C) and leave until dried but not coloured. Turn the tray if necessary. Cooking time will be approximately 3 hours.

5 When cooked, leave to cool, remove from tray. Mix together the icing ingredients, and pipe on nose, eyes, mouth and buttons.

YOU WILL NEED:
3 egg whites
150 g (6 oz) caster sugar
Chocolate icing:
50 g (2 oz) icing sugar
1 teaspoonful cocoa powder
2–3 (10–15 ml) tea-spoonfuls hot water
1 sheet of waxed or parchment paper (to line baking trays)

Easter Party

Rabbit Cake

Cheese and Peanut Whirls

Savouries

Sausage Fingers

Viking Jellies

Rabbit Cake

YOU WILL NEED:

200 g (8 oz) margarine
  or butter
200 g (8 oz) caster sugar
4 eggs
300 g (12 oz) self raising
  flour
Almond flavouring
  (optional)
100 – 150 g (4 – 6 oz)
  lemon curd
100 – 150 g (4 – 6 oz)
  desiccated coconut

50 g (2 oz) marzipan
  and small sweets
1 cake case
Cocktail sticks
Roll of liquorice
  ribbon
1 × 1 pint (500 ml)
  ovenproof basin
1 × 1½ pint (750 ml)
  ovenproof basin

1 Make cake mixture, using the creaming method.
Place margarine in a mixing bowl and soften with a
wooden spoon. Add the sugar, and cream together
until light and fluffy.

2 Beat eggs in a small bowl with a fork.

3 Add beaten eggs a tablespoonful at a time to the creamed margarine and sugar, beating very well with a wooden spoon.

4 Add flavouring if used.

5 Sift in the flour, and mix in very lightly with a spoon.

6 Grease the ovenproof basins. Stand these on a baking tray with the cake case.

7 Place 1 teaspoonful of cake mixture into case, and put two-thirds of the remaining mixture into one basin and the rest into the second.

8 Place on the middle shelf of a moderately hot oven, Gas Mark 4 (electricity 350°F/180°C). The cake in the cake case will take 15 minutes, the larger cake approximately 45 minutes, and the largest 60 minutes. The cakes will be springy to the touch and beginning to shrink slightly from the side of the bowls when cooked. Test with a skewer.

TO DECORATE

1 After cooling slightly, remove from the basins and place on a cooling rack.

2 When cool, fit cakes together, place largest cake round side uppermost on a plate or cakeboard (trim base of cake if required). Place other cake on top, again round side uppermost, and trim base round to look like a head. Small cake in cake case can be cut to make tail.

3 Spread cakes all over with lemon curd, then dip into coconut. (Place coconut on a sheet of greaseproof paper.)

4 Shape 2 ears from marzipan, and secure in cake with cocktail sticks.

5 Add eyes and nose, using either marzipan or small sweets.

6 Place liquorice ribbon round neck.

7 If wished, a small amount of coconut can be coloured green to use as grass.

Cheese & Peanut Whirls

1 Sift flour and pepper.

2 Cut margarine into small pieces, and rub into flour with fingertips until there are no large pieces.

3 Add grated cheese and chopped peanuts, and mix in well.

4 Beat egg and milk together in a small basin, add to the ingredients in the bowl, and mix in with a fork to a soft dough.

5 Using one hand, gently knead the dough.

6 Turn out onto floured work surface and roll to an oblong 25 cm × 30 cm (10 in × 12 in).

7 Roll up the longest side and divide into twelve pieces.

8 Place on a lightly greased baking sheet.

9 Bake for 10 minutes at Gas Mark 6 (electricity 400°F/200°C).

YOU WILL NEED:

200 g (8 oz) self raising flour

50 g (2 oz) margarine

1 egg

2–3 tablespoonfuls milk

75 g (3 oz) grated Cheddar or Leicester cheese

50 g (2 oz) chopped salted peanuts

Pinch of pepper

12½ g (½ oz) flour for rolling

If wished, the tops of the whirls can be brushed with beaten egg before baking.

Savouries

Savouries for children must look as appetising as they are nutritious, but must also be easy and convenient to eat. They can be based on savoury biscuits or crackers as well as bread.

TOPPINGS

1 Grated cheese mixed with a mild sweet pickle/chutney.
2 Hardboiled or scrambled egg, and chopped ham.
3 Salmon and sliced cucumber.
4 Liver and bacon spread.
  Gently fry 100 g (4 oz) chopped lamb's liver together with 1 rasher chopped bacon and 25 g (1 oz) margarine for 10 minutes. Add pepper and a little tomato sauce to taste. Mash the mixture well in a small basin, allow to cool, and spread as required.

Sausage Fingers

1 Make shortcrust pastry, using the rubbing-in method. Sift flour and salt. Add fats, cut up into small pieces, and rub in with the fingertips until the mixture looks like breadcrumbs. Add the water, mix in with a knife, and gather together to make a soft (but not sticky) dough.

2 Divide dough into two.

3 Roll out each piece of dough to an oblong about 15 cm × 25 cm (6 in × 10 in). Place one piece on a flat baking tray. Press the sausage meat on top of this to within ½ cm (¼ in) of all edges. (If wished, finely chopped onion can be added to the sausage meat when spreading it on the pastry.) Brush edge of pastry with beaten egg. Place remaining pastry on top. Seal and decorate edges, score top with a knife.

YOU WILL NEED:
300 g (12 oz) plain flour
75 g (3 oz) margarine
75 g (3 oz) lard
Pinch of salt
12 teaspoonfuls or 4 tablespoonfuls cold water
300 g (12 oz) sausage meat
Beaten egg to glaze/seal
Flour for rolling

4 Brush with beaten egg.

5 Place on top shelf in oven. Bake at Gas Mark 6 (electricity 400°F/ 200°C) for 30 minutes.

6 Allow to cool. Cut into fingers, and remove carefully from the tin.

Viking Jellies

If wished, a layer of fruit can be placed on top of the jellies before adding the icecream.

YOU WILL NEED:

1 flavoured jelly
3 bananas
6 tall glasses
1 small block icecream
Grated chocolate
Allow 2 hours setting time in a cool place.

1 Place the broken jelly tablet in a measuring jug, add 125 ml (¼ pt) boiling water, stir to dissolve. When completely dissolved add ice-cubes and cold water to bring up to 500 ml (1 pt). This will bring down the temperature quickly and speed up the setting time. Pour into the glasses, leave in a cool place to set.

2 When set, cut bananas in half and cut again lengthways.

3 Place a spoonful of icecream on top of the jelly and sprinkle with grated chocolate. Top with bananas so that they stand out of the top of the glass. Serve at once.

Hallowe'en and Bonfire Night Party

Pigs in Blankets

Jacket Potatoes

Witches Brew Soup

Devilled Fish Pinwheel

Chocolate Fingers

Slab Apple Cake

Warming, easy-to-eat, 'no fuss' food is ideal for cold frosty evenings.

Pigs in Blankets

YOU WILL NEED:

100 g (4 oz) self raising flour
50 g (2 oz) margarine
50 g (2 oz) grated cheese
1 beaten egg
1 tablespoonful (15 ml) cold water
Salt and pepper
1 teaspoonful chopped dried parsley
Flour for rolling
200 g (8 oz) skinless sausages

1 Sift flour, salt and pepper into a mixing bowl.

2 Cut fat into small pieces and rub in with fingertips.

3 Add the grated cheese and dried parsley.

4 Mix 1 tablespoonful of beaten egg and 1 tablespoonful of water together, add to dry ingredients, and mix to a soft (but not sticky) dough.

5 Turn onto a lightly floured surface, and knead gently.

6 Roll to an oblong ½ cm (¼ in) thick. Trim edges.

7 Cut into 3 strips lengthways, about 3 cm (1¼ in) narrower than the sausages.

8 Brush the pastry strips with the remaining beaten egg.

9 Wrap the sausages in the pastry, roll over and overlap by 1 cm (½ in). Cut off the pastry.

10 Repeat for all sausages.

11 Place on baking sheet, joined edges underneath, and score tops with knife. Brush with beaten egg. Bake 15 minutes on middle shelf, Gas Mark 6 (electricity 400°F/200°C). Any pastry trimmings can be re-rolled and cut as biscuits or for decoration.

Jacket Potatoes

On bonfire night, baked potatoes can be cooked in the embers of the fire. The safest way is to wrap in foil before cooking.

Pages 9–10 give ideas for baking and serving from the oven.

Witches Brew Soup

1 Make up the soups in a large saucepan, following the packet instructions.

2 Add the pasta and heat —simmer 5 to 10 minutes according to type.

3 Serve with bread chunks.

YOU WILL NEED:
1 pkt tomato soup
1 pkt beef and onion, or oxtail, soup
50 g (2 oz) pasta shapes
Bread to serve

Devilled Fish Pinwheel

1 Roll out pastry to 30 cm (12 in) square. Trim. Place on a baking sheet.

2 Mix filling ingredients together in a small basin, mashing well.

3 Place filling in centre of pastry. Cut in from the corners just to the filling. Moisten outside

YOU WILL NEED:
200 g (8 oz) pkt flaky or rough puff pastry
Flour for rolling
Filling:
175 g (7 oz) tuna fish
1 teaspoonful curry powder
2 teaspoonfuls vinegar or lemon juice
Egg glaze

edges of pastry with cold water. Fold over tips as shown (ABCD to centre). Glaze with egg, and decorate edges. Bake at Gas Mark 6 (electricity 400°F/200°C) for 25 minutes on top shelf.

To make individual pinwheels, roll, as for stage 1, then divide into four. Continue from stage 2.

Chocolate Fingers

YOU WILL NEED:

100 g (4 oz) margarine
25 g (1 oz) sugar
1 level tablespoonful
   golden syrup
100 g (4 oz) self raising flour
12½ g (½ oz) cocoa powder
50 g (2 oz) coconut
50 g (2 oz) raisins or sultanas
50 g (2 oz) rolled oats
18 cm (7 in) square
   cake tin, greased

1 Place margarine, sugar and golden syrup in small pan and melt together, stirring gently, then leave to cool slightly. Add cocoa powder.

2 Mix in the self raising flour, then add oats, fruit and coconut and stir. Place in tin, press down well.

3 Bake at Gas Mark 4 (electricity 350°F/180°C) for 30 minutes on middle shelf. Remove from oven, cool slightly and cut into pieces.

Slab Apple Cake

1 Grease the cake tin, and line the base with a piece of greaseproof paper.

2 Peel, quarter and slice the apples, and place in a pan, adding 2 tablespoonfuls water. Place the lid on the pan and cook very gently for 3 – 4 minutes until apples just begin to soften. Remove from the heat, and add the sugar and cinnamon.

Leave to cool.

YOU WILL NEED:

200 g (8 oz) self raising flour

100 g (4 oz) margarine

100 g (4 oz) brown sugar

2 eggs

2 tablespoonfuls milk

Apple filling:

400 g (1 lb) cooking apples

1 level teaspoonful cinnamon (optional)

50 g (2 oz) granulated sugar

25 g (1 oz) brown sugar

Deep 20 cm (8 in) cake tin

3 Sift flour into a mixing bowl. Add margarine cut up into small pieces and rub in with fingertips. Add sugar.

4 Beat eggs and milk, and mix into dry ingredients with a wooden spoon.

5 Place half the mixture in the base of the tin.

6 Spread apple filling on top of the base. Top with remaining mixture, sprinkle with the 25 g (1 oz) brown sugar.

7 Bake in a moderate oven, Gas Mark 4 (electricity 350°F/180°C) for 60 minutes until firm in centre and golden brown.

8 Allow to cool completely before slicing into fingers. Can be served buttered.

Pizza Party

Pizza

Chess Board Sandwiches

Coleslaw

Orange and Pineapple Sorbet

Pizza

YOU WILL NEED:

Bread Base

300 g (12 oz)
   wholewheat
   or strong white
   plain flour

25 g (1 oz) lard

12½ g (½ oz) fresh
   yeast or 1 level
   tablespoonful dried
   yeast

166 ml (⅓ pt) warm
   water

1 teaspoonful sugar

1 teaspoonful salt

Topping

50 g (2 oz) mushrooms

1 small tin tomatoes

150 – 200 g (6 – 8 oz)
   grated cheese

1 very finely chopped
   onion

50 g (2 oz) chopped
   ham or bacon

250 ml (½ pt) milk

25 g (1 oz) plain flour

25 g (1 oz) margarine

Salt and pepper

Baking trays

1 Make up bread dough for base:
   Put 166 ml (⅓ pt) warm water in a measuring jug,
   add sugar and yeast and stir. Place flour and salt
   in a large mixing bowl. Rub in fat with fingertips.

2 Add dissolved yeast liquid all at once and stir to
   make a soft dough; knead in the bowl for 2 – 3
   minutes. Cover and leave in a warm place to
   rise – approximately 30 minutes.

3 Whilst dough is rising, make a sauce using milk, flour, margarine and salt and pepper. Melt the margarine on a low heat, then remove from heat, stir in the flour, and gradually add the milk. Return to heat, and bring to the boil, stirring with a wooden spoon. Boil for 1 minute. Add salt and pepper to taste.

4 Re-knead the dough – turn onto a work surface and knead well for 5 minutes. If individual pizzas rather than one large one are required, divide dough into 6 round pieces and roll to the size of a saucer. Place well apart on greased baking sheets.

5 Spread the sauce on the dough and top with a little tomato, sliced mushroom, and chopped onion. Sprinkle with grated cheese, and top with ham or bacon.

6 Leave in a warm place for a further 30 minutes to rise.

7 Bake in a hot oven, Gas Mark 7 (electricity 425°F/220°C) for 20 – 25 minutes small, 35 – 40 minutes large. Serve.

The bread dough base can be used to make rolls or loaves.

Chess Board Sandwiches

YOU WILL NEED:

Sliced brown bread
Sliced white bread
Butter or margarine

Fillings:

a) *Chopped hardboiled egg and cress*
b) *Grated cheese and apple*
c) *Cream cheese and finely chopped cucumber*
d) *Tinned fish (salmon, tuna or mackerel), with lemon juice or mayonnaise*
e) *Mashed banana and brown sugar*
f) *Peanut butter*

Slices of tomato, cucumber, egg and lettuce for decoration.

1 Soften the butter or margarine, using a knife, and then lightly spread on bread slices.

2 Spread the fillings on half of the number of slices. Top with the other slices.

3 Trim off all crusts, and cut each sandwich into 9 squares.

4 Arrange on a flat board, alternating brown and white squares.

5 Garnish and serve.

Coleslaw

1 Remove outer leaves from cabbage and discard.

2 Shred very finely, using a sharp knife, and place in a bowl.

3 Peel and finely chop onion
Peel and grate carrot } add to bowl

4 Peel and grate apple

5 Mix well together in the bowl, add salad cream to taste. Stir in well and serve.

YOU WILL NEED:
¼ white cabbage
1 small onion
1 large carrot
1 dessert apple
Salad cream or
mayonnaise

Orange and Pineapple Sorbet

1 Place pineapple and its juice in a measuring jug, and make up with water to 500 ml (1 pt).

YOU WILL NEED:
Large tin crushed
pineapple
75 g (3 oz) sugar
Juice of 2 oranges
2 egg whites
Water

2 Place in a pan with the sugar, bring to boil, and boil rapidly for 3 minutes.

3 Cool, then add orange juice, and place in a shallow dish and freeze until just 'mushy'.

4 Whisk egg whites stiffly and fold into the half-set fruit.

5 Return to freezer and freeze through. Serve.

Birthday Party

Triple Deckers

Cheese and Pickle Parcels

Nut Crunch Cookies

Chocolate Cat Cake

Strawberry Trifle

Triple Deckers

YOU WILL NEED:
Brown or white bread – 4 slices of bread for
each round of sandwiches; butter or margarine

Fillings:

(i) a *Banana mashed with a little honey* – or
     b *Peanut butter*

(ii) a *Cream cheese and chopped pineapple or chives* – or
      b *Cottage cheese and sultanas* – or
      c *Grated cheese and apple or mild sweet pickle*

(iii) a *Hardboiled or scrambled egg and cress* – or
       b *Tinned fish mashed with a little lemon juice*
          or vinegar – or
       c *Cooked ham*

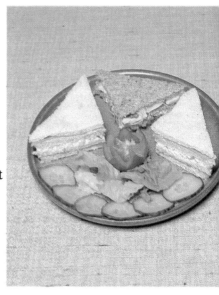

1 Spread one side of each slice of bread with butter or margarine.

2 Top three with a different filling, varying sweet and savoury flavours.

3 Assemble as shown, finishing with the last slice of bread and butter.

4 Cut each round into fingers or cut into 4 diagonally. Trim off crusts if wished.

Cheese and Pickle Parcels

1 Roll pastry out to a square 30 cm × 30 cm (12 in × 12 in). Trim edges.

2 Cut into 16 equal-sized squares. Place 8 pieces on a flat baking tray.

3 Divide the filling equally between the squares, placing it carefully in the centre.

4 Brush the edges of filled squares with beaten egg, and top with the other pastry squares. Brush tops with beaten egg.

5 Seal edges with a fork to decorate.

6 Bake for 10 – 15 minutes on top shelf at Gas Mark 7 (electricity 425°F/220°C) until golden brown.

YOU WILL NEED:
200 g (8 oz) flaky or rough puff pastry
1 beaten egg

Filling:

150 g (6 oz) grated cheese } *Mix together*
1 tablespoonful sweet pickle

Nut Crunch Cookies

YOU WILL NEED:

100 g (4 oz) margarine
50 g (2 oz) caster sugar
1 tablespoonful of golden syrup 75 g (3 oz)
1 tablespoonful of black treacle 75 g (3 oz)
1 egg

150 g (6 oz) wholewheat flour (or 75 g (3 oz) plain flour and 75 g (3 oz) rolled oats)
25 g (1 oz) currants or raisins
50 g (2 oz) blanched chopped almonds or walnuts

1 Cream together margarine and sugar.

2 Beat in the egg, then gradually beat in the golden syrup and black treacle.

3 Add the dried fruit and chopped nuts.

4 Gradually work in the flour.

5 Place teaspoonfuls of the mixture well apart on a greased baking tray, pressing down lightly with a fork.

6 Bake on middle shelf of oven for 15 minutes at Gas Mark 4 (electricity 350°F/180°C), until edges are just firm.

7 Remove from baking tray, and cool on a wire rack.

Store in an airtight tin.

Chocolate Cat Cake

YOU WILL NEED:
150 g (6 oz) margarine
150 g (6 oz) caster sugar
3 eggs
150 g (6 oz) self
  raising flour
25 g (1 oz) cocoa

Chocolate water icing:
200 g (8 oz) icing sugar
1 level tablespoon
  12½ g (½ oz) cocoa
25 g (1 oz) desiccated
  coconut

Decoration:
Liquorice sticks and sweets

1 Make up cake mixture, using the creaming method. Cream margarine and sugar until light and fluffy.

2 Break the eggs into a small basin.

3 Add the beaten egg gradually to the creamed mixture, a tablespoonful at a time, beating well with a wooden spoon.

4 Sift flour and cocoa together, and fold into creamed mixture as lightly as possible, using a metal spoon or spatula.

5 Divide between two greased and lined 18 cm (7 in) shallow cake tins.

6 Bake on the middle shelf of a moderate oven, Gas Mark 4 (electricity 350°F/180°C) for 20–25 minutes until well-risen and firm to the touch.

7 Remove from the tins, and cool on a cooling rack covered by a damp tea-towel.

8 Cut as shown, and re-assemble on a serving board.

Make up chocolate water icing: mix cocoa and icing sugar, add warm water and coconut, and spread on to cake. Add eyes from liquorice sweets. Make whiskers from a liquorice coil.

Strawberry Trifle

YOU WILL NEED:

*1 pkt fruit flavoured
    jelly (raspberry
    or strawberry)
1 small tin strawberries
1 pkt strawberry
    blancmange powder
500 ml (1 pt) milk
25 g (1 oz) sugar
125 ml (¼ pt) double or
    whipping cream
Ice-cubes
Individual dishes
Grated chocolate*

1 Place broken jelly tablet in a measuring jug, pour
    on 125 ml (¼ pt) boiling water, and stir to
    dissolve. When completely dissolved, add ice-
    cubes to make up to 375 ml (¾ pt). Add the
    contents of the tin of fruit including juice. Divide
    between individual dishes, and leave in a cool
    place to set.

2 Make up blancmange according to packet
    instructions, and leave to cool.

3 When jelly is set and blancmange just warm,
    spoon the blancmange on top of the jelly. Leave
    until cold.

4 When cooled and set, whisk cream until stiff
    enough to stand in peaks, and spoon on the top
    of each trifle.

5 Decorate with grated chocolate and serve.

Toddlers Birthday Party

Sandwiches
❧
Alphabet Biscuits
❧
Orange Jelly
❧
Kiddie Cakes
❧
Teddy Bear Cake

Sandwiches

Choose familiar foods to use as sandwich fillings.

After making, cut into small shapes, or roll and slice.

Fillings:

Scrambled egg and cress
Cheese spread

Savoury fingers:

Spread warm toast with a little butter, then spread thinly with Marmite. Remove crusts and cut into fingers.

Alphabet Biscuits

1 Sift flour into a bowl, add ground rice and sugar.

2 Cut butter into small pieces and rub into flour with fingertips, gradually working the dough together.

YOU WILL NEED:

125 g (5 oz) plain flour
25 g (1 oz) ground rice
75 g (3 oz) sugar
75 g (3 oz) butter
250 g (10 oz) icing sugar
8 × 5 ml teaspoonfuls cold water
Few drops of food colouring
Flour for rolling
Biscuit cutters

3 Turn onto a lightly floured surface, and roll out to
  ½ cm (¼ in) thick. Cut out, using animal cutters.
  Place on a baking sheet and bake at Gas Mark 3
  (electricity 325°F/160°C) for 15 minutes until just
  firm. Remove from tray and cool on a wire rack.

ICING

1 Sift icing sugar into a bowl, and add water,
  measuring accurately. Mix to a consistency that will
  coat the back of the wooden spoon quite thickly.

2 Remove 1 tablespoonful icing and place in a small
  basin. Add a few drops of food colouring. Place
  this icing in an icing bag fitted with a plain writing
  nozzle.

Place 1 teaspoonful of the uncoloured icing onto each biscuit, then pipe on the coloured icing in the letters of the alphabet. Alternatively, biscuits could have the initials of children's names on them.

Orange Jelly

Make up jelly following the instructions but replacing 125 ml (¼ pt) of the water with the orange juice. Set in individual dishes. Serve with icecream.

YOU WILL NEED:
1 orange jelly
Juice of 2 oranges

YOU WILL NEED:

75 g (3 oz) margarine   75 g (3 oz) self raising flour
75 g (3 oz) caster sugar   24 – 30 petit four cake cases
1 large egg (size 2)

1 Cream margarine and sugar together, beating with wooden spoon until light and fluffy.

2 Add egg gradually.

3 Fold in flour with a metal spoon.

4 Arrange cake cases well apart on baking trays.

5 Place a small amount of mixture in each case.

6 Place on the middle shelf of a moderate oven, Gas Mark 4 (electricity 350°F/180°C) for 10 minutes, until well-risen and golden brown.

DECORATIONS

1 *100 g (4 oz) icing sugar*
4 × 5 ml teaspoonfuls water or *orange juice (with 2 – 3 drops of food colouring)*

Top each cake with icing; add hundreds and thousands, or chocolate buttons/flake etc.

2 *1 tablespoonful seedless jam*
1 tablespoonful desiccated coconut, few pieces of glacé cherry

Warm jam slightly and brush onto each cake, then sprinkle with coconut and add piece of cherry.

3 *100 g (4 oz) chocolate, few coloured sweets*

Place chocolate in a basin over a pan of hot water. When melted, place a small amount on top of each cake, and top with coloured sweets.

Teddy Bear Cake

Cake recipe as Cat cake (omitting cocoa)

Cut cake

ORANGE BUTTER ICING

200 g (8 oz) icing sugar

100 g (4 oz) margarine

15 ml (1 tbsp) orange juice

25 g (1 oz) desiccated coconut (to sprinkle)

Chocolate buttons

Liquorice ribbon

Picnic Party

Savoury Tarts

Lemon Squares

Drinks

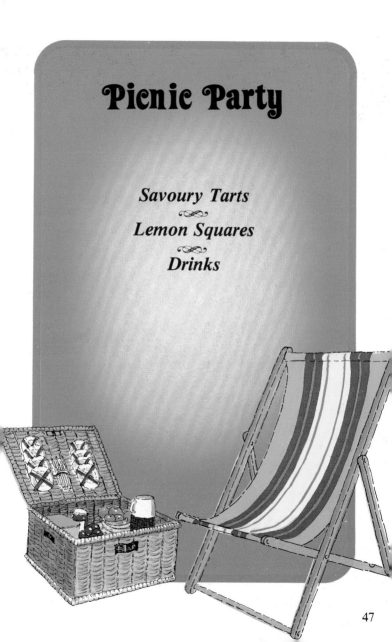

When eating outside, food needs to be easy to pack and serve with limited equipment. Containers with well fitting lids for liquids are useful.

Savoury Tarts

Cheese pastry – *YOU WILL NEED:*
200g (8oz) plain/wholewheat flour
50g (2oz) lard
50g (2oz) margarine
50g (2oz) grated cheese
Salt and pepper
1 egg yolk
1½ – 2 tablespoonfuls cold water

1 Sift flour, salt and pepper, and rub in fats. Add grated cheese, and mix in well.

2 Mix egg yolk with water, and add to rubbed-in mixture, mixing with knife. Knead dough together, using one hand.

3 Roll out on lightly floured board. Cut into 15–18 rounds, using a pastry cutter slightly larger than the rim of the patty tins.

4 Prick pastry well with a fork.

5 Bake empty shells for 5 minutes at Gas Mark 7 (electricity 425°F/220°C) until just firm.

Fillings

CORNED BEEF AND
ONION (makes 12)

1 Peel and chop onion,
   and fry lightly in
   margarine until just
   soft.

2 Chop corned beef.

3 Mix all ingredients
   together in a small
   basin. Divide between pastry cases.

4 Bake at Gas Mark 5 (electricity 375°F/190°C) for
   15 – 20 minutes until just set.

YOU WILL NEED:

1 large egg
125 ml (¼ pt) milk
Salt and pepper
1 onion
25 g (1 oz) margarine
100 g (4 oz) corned beef

CHEESE AND MIXED
VEGETABLE (makes 12)

1 Mix all ingredients
   together and divide
   between the pastry
   cases.

2 Bake at Gas Mark 5
   (electricity
   375°F/190°C) for
   15 – 20 minutes until
   just set.

YOU WILL NEED:

1 large egg
125 ml (¼ pt) milk
100 g (4 oz) grated
  cheese
Salt and pepper
100 g (4 oz) cooked
  mixed vegetables

Other savoury tarts can be made using prawns, or
pink salmon, or mushrooms and bacon.

Serve with potato salad and coleslaw, whole
tomatoes and celery sticks.

All can be packed in plastic boxes.

Lemon Squares

1 Grease a 20 cm (8 in) square shallow cake tin.

2 Cream margarine and sugar until light and fluffy.

3 Break eggs into a small bowl and beat together.

4 Beat eggs gradually into the creamed mixture.

5 Stir in the grated lemon rind.

6 Gently fold in the flour.

7 Place in the cake tin and bake for 25 – 30 minutes at Gas Mark 4 (electricity 350°F/ 180°C) until just firm.

8 Mix lemon juice with caster sugar, and pour onto cake whilst still hot. Leave in tin to cool.

9 Serve cut into fingers.

YOU WILL NEED:
100 g (4 oz) margarine
125 g (5 oz) sugar
150 g (6 oz) self raising flour
Grated rind of 2 lemons
2 large eggs

Topping:
Juice of 2 lemons
100 g (4 oz) caster sugar

As an alternative, serve a selection of fresh fruit with fingers of mild cheese.

Drinks need to be icy cold or piping hot. For either, a vacuum flask is ideal.

Drinks

Milk Shakes

YOU WILL NEED:

For each person:

250 ml (½ pt) milk (chilled)

1 level dessertspoonful sugar or to taste

Ice-cubes (optional)

Icecream

Flavourings:

2 teaspoonfuls cocoa powder

or *1 ripe banana*

or *50 g (2 oz) strawberries*

(Alternatively, milk shake syrups or powders may be used.)

Place milk flavouring and sugar in a mixing bowl and whisk very well until frothy. Pour into glasses. Top with icecream. If a liquidiser is available, milk, sugar, flavouring and ice-cubes can be liquidised together for 30 seconds, then topped with icecream as before.

Lemon Drink

YOU WILL NEED:

500 ml (1 pt) cold milk

2 – 3 tablespoonfuls lemon curd

1 tablespoonful lime cordial

A few drops of yellow food colouring

Tall glasses

Whisk lemon curd, lime cordial, food colouring, and milk together. Pour into tall glasses and serve.